Question Time

Human Body

Angela Wilkes

KING*f*ISHER

Editor: Carron Brown
Designer: Rebecca Johns
DTP manager: Nicky Studdart
Consultants: Richard Walker, Norah Granger
Indexer: Jason Hook
Production controller: Caroline Hansell
Illustrators: Roger Stuart 4–5, 8–9, 14–15, 28–29; **Alan Hancock**
29*tr*; **Jonathan Potter/Wildlife** 26*bc*, 26*cr*, 27*l*; **Mike Saunders**
22–23*c*; **Guy Smith** 6–7, 10–11, 12–13, 16–17, 18*b*, 19*tl*, 21*tl*, 23*tl*,
24–25, 26*bl*, 27*bc*.
Cartoons: Ian Dicks
Picture research manager: Jane Lambert
Picture acknowledgements: 5*tr* Corbis; **7***cr* Science Photo
Library/Clinical Radiology Dept., Salisbury District Hospital; **13***tr*
Science Photo Library/Princess Margaret Rose Orthopaedic Hospital;
15*tc* gettyone/Stone/Frank Siteman; **17***cr* Corbis; **19***cr* Science Photo
Library/Mark Clarke; **21***cr* Corbis; **23***c* Corbis; **27***cr* Corbis.

Every effort has been made to trace the copyright holders of the photographs.
The publishers apologise for any inconvenience caused.

KINGFISHER
Kingfisher Publications Plc
New Penderel House,
283–288 High Holborn,
London WC1V 7HZ
www.kingfisherpub.com

First published by Kingfisher Publications Plc 2001
10 9 8 7 6 5 4 3 2 1

1TR/0401/TIM/RNB/NA128

A CIP catalogue record for
this book is available from
the British Library.

ISBN 0 7534 0628 4

Printed in China

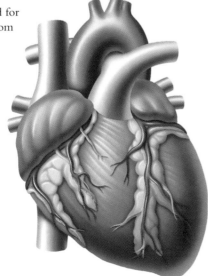

CONTENTS

ABOUT this book

Have you ever wondered what makes you blink? On every page, find out the answers to questions like this and other fascinating facts about the human body. Words in **bold** are explained in the glossary on page 31.

Look and Find
★ sweat gland ★

All through the book you will see the **Look and Find** symbol. This has the name and picture of a small object that is hidden somewhere on the page. Look carefully to see if you can find it.

Now I Know...

★ This box contains quick answers to all of the questions.
★ They will help you remember all about the amazing human body.

Look and Find ★ ear

WHY do we look different?

People around the world are many different shapes and sizes. They may be short or tall, thin or plump. The colour of their skin and hair can range from very fair to very dark. A person's appearance depends on their age, sex and what other members of their family look like. It may even be affected by the work they do. But, beneath the skin, everyone's body works in exactly the same way.

WHAT are the main parts of the body?

Head

Chest

Arm

Abdomen

Leg

All bodies are made of the same basic parts. Your head is at the top of your body. The trunk of your body has two parts: the chest in the upper half and the **abdomen** in the lower half. Your two arms and two legs make up your four limbs.

That's Amazing!

No two fingerprints are the same!

Babies cannot talk, so they cry to let people know they want something!

HOW do you communicate?

People communicate mainly by talking and listening to each other. You have a voice that your family and friends know at once, but you can communicate in other ways too. When people talk to you, they look at your face. This is because your smile and other facial expressions show what you are feeling. You also use body language such as pointing and waving.

People who are deaf have difficulty hearing. They can communicate with sign language, using hand signs and facial expressions for certain words.

Now I Know...

★ People all look different but their bodies all work the same way.
★ All bodies are made up of a head, chest, abdomen and limbs.
★ You communicate mainly by talking and listening.

5

WHAT is inside your body?

Your body is like a very complicated piece of machinery. It is made up of thousands of different parts all tightly packed together beneath your skin. Important body parts, such as **muscles**, bones and other **organs**, are controlled by **nerves** and supplied by tubes that carry blood to them. These hidden parts of your body work non-stop, all day and night, to keep you alive, give you energy and make you grow.

HOW does your body work?

Inside your body there are several different systems that work alongside each other. Each system is made up of a group of organs. These are all joined together to carry out an important job, such as transporting **oxygen**, moving bones or **digesting** food. The different systems all work together smoothly to keep your body working properly.

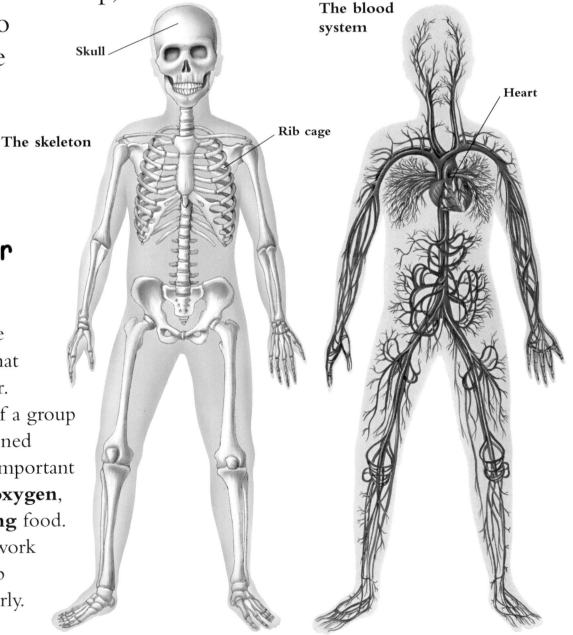

The blood system

Skull

Heart

The skeleton

Rib cage

WHERE are your main organs?

Most of your body's main organs are inside your head, chest and abdomen. Your liver is in the upper abdomen. Close by are two kidneys, one on either side of your spine. Bones protect many of the organs from damage. Your brain is hidden inside the skull that forms your head. In your chest, your heart and lungs are protected by the rib cage.

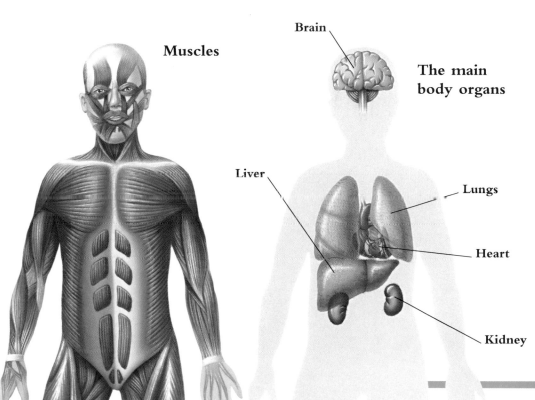

Muscles

Brain

The main body organs

Liver

Lungs

Heart

Kidney

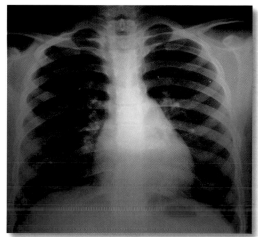

This **X-ray** of a chest shows the heart (in the middle) and lungs (the dark areas at either side of the heart), inside the rib cage.

Now I Know...

★ There are thousands of different body parts under your skin.

★ Several body systems work together inside you.

★ Your main organs are deep inside you, protected by bones.

WHY is skin different colours?

Your skin covers your whole body. It is stretchy and fits you like a glove. Some people have pale skin and others have dark skin. This is because skin has brown colouring in it called melanin. If your skin has a lot of melanin, you will have darker skin than someone whose skin has a small amount. Melanin protects your body from the Sun's harmful rays. If you spend a lot of time in the Sun, your skin makes more melanin and you get a suntan.

WHAT makes people sweat?

Sweating helps you to stay at an even temperature. Coiled tubes, called sweat glands, deep in your skin make watery sweat. Beads of sweat rise to the surface of your skin through tiny holes called **pores**. The sweat **evaporates** and this helps to cool you down.

When you exercise, you get hot and this makes you sweat.

Light-skinned people need to wear sun-tan cream to stop the Sun's rays burning their skin.

HOW do you feel pain?

Your skin gives you your sense of touch. Beneath its wafer-thin surface there is a layer called the **dermis**. This is packed with tiny nerve endings that send messages to your brain when you touch things. Some nerve endings react to pressure, heat and cold, or movement. Others detect pain. The dermis contains oil glands that make oils to keep your skin soft. There are also hair follicles – pits in the skin from which your hairs grow.

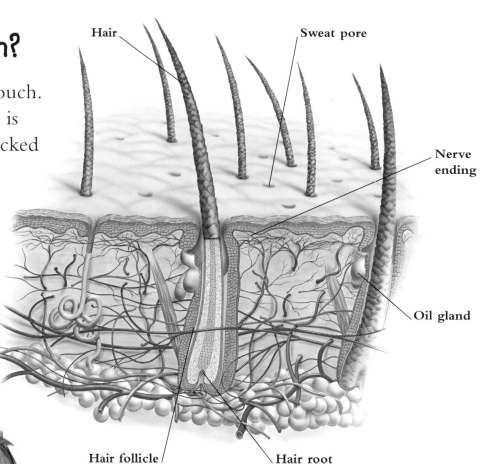

Hair

Sweat pore

Nerve ending

Oil gland

Hair follicle

Hair root

That's Amazing!

If you had no skin, your insides would dry out like a prune!

You lose and replace about 90 hairs a day!

Now I Know...

★ Skin has brown colouring in it called melanin that gives your skin colour.
★ Skin makes watery sweat to help your body cool down.
★ Skin contains nerve endings that give you your sense of touch.

WHAT does your brain do?

Your brain is an organ inside your skull about as big as your two fists. Yet it is more complex than any computer and controls your whole body. It is where you think, have feelings and ideas, learn things and store memories. It also keeps every part of your body working. The brain is divided into many different areas, each of which controls the different things you do, say, think, feel and see.

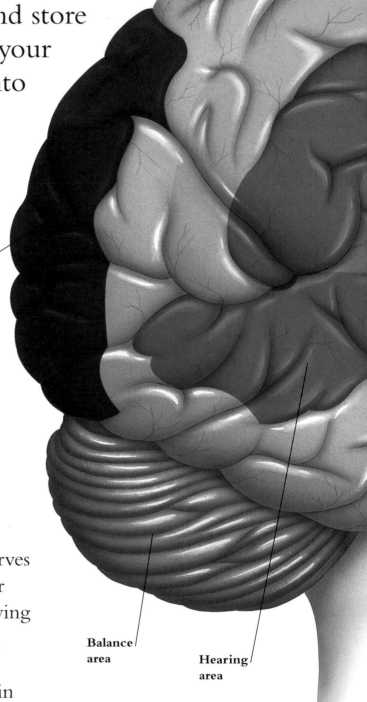

The nervous system

Spinal cord

Sight area

Balance area

Hearing area

HOW is your brain linked to the rest of your body?

Your brain is made of billions of linked nerve **cells**. It is joined to the rest of your body by the spinal cord – a long bundle of nerves that runs down the centre of your spine. Nerves are like wires carrying tiny electrical signals that flash to the brain and back again. They branch out from the spinal cord to every part of your body. Your brain and nerves make up your nervous system.

The right half of the brain

Touch area

Movement area

Talking area (usually on the left half of your brain)

Thinking, personality and emotions area (front of your brain)

Any one cell in your brain may be connected to as many as 10,000 other brain cells!

Signals flash between the brain and nerves at speeds of up to 400 km per hour!

WHY doesn't your body stop working when you go to sleep?

Your brain works automatically day and night, so your body keeps working even when you are fast asleep. The brain stem at the base of your brain links your brain to the spinal cord. It controls many things without you having to think about them, such as how fast your heart beats and how often you breathe.

Now I Know...

★ The brain is the control centre for the whole of your body.

★ Your brain is linked to your body by the spinal cord and nerves.

★ Your brain works automatically day and night.

11

Look and Find
★ ★
elbow joint

WHY do you have bones?

There are more than 206 bones inside you; all joined together they make up your skeleton. Your skeleton gives your body support and shape – without it, you would collapse in a heap. Bones are different sizes and shapes, depending on the weight they support and the work they do. Your thigh bones are the largest bones in your body. They are long and strong to support the weight of your body whenever you stand up, run, walk or jump.

That's Amazing!

Nearly half the bones in your body are in your hands, feet, wrists and ankles!

You have exactly the same number of neck bones as a giraffe!

HOW do bones fit together?

Most of your bones are linked by joints so they can move in different directions. The knee joint is where the curved bottom end of the thigh bone fits into the curved top end of the shin bone. The ends of the bones are covered in slippery fluid so your knee can move backwards and forwards smoothly.

The skeleton

Knee joint

Hip joint

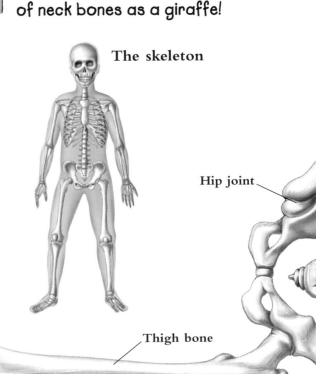

Ankle joint

Shin bone

Knee-cap

Thigh bone

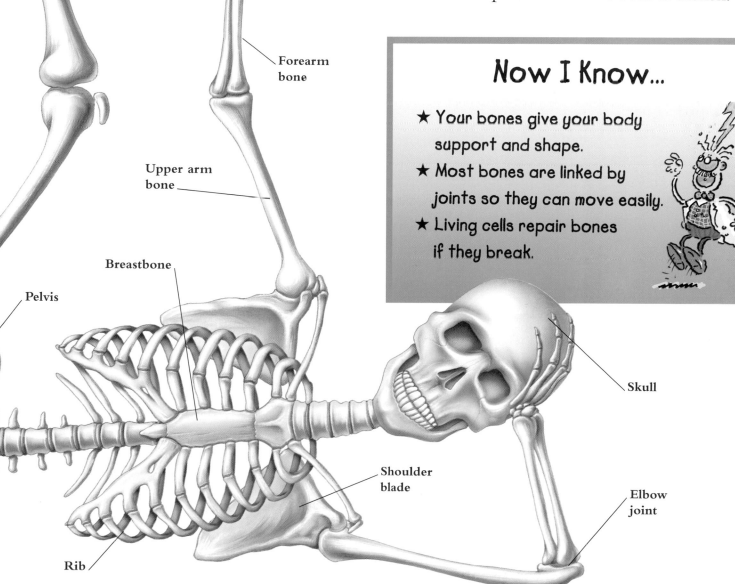

Foot bones

Hand bones

Wrist joint

Forearm bone

Upper arm bone

Breastbone

Pelvis

Shoulder blade

Rib

Skull

Elbow joint

WHAT happens if you break a bone?

Bones contain living cells that help them grow longer and stronger as you grow. If you break a bone, the cells repair the damage and the bone mends itself. Sometimes, a doctor sets the broken bone in a hard plaster cast to stop it from moving. This helps the bone to mend in the correct position.

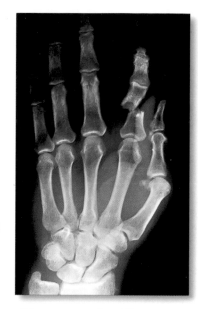

Doctors take X-ray photographs to see if a bone is broken.

Now I Know...

★ Your bones give your body support and shape.

★ Most bones are linked by joints so they can move easily.

★ Living cells repair bones if they break.

WHAT makes you move?

Every movement you make, from a blink to a jump, is made by muscles. You have over 600 different muscles. Many of them are attached to your bones by strong, rope-like bands called tendons that allow you to move every part of your body. There are also muscles in your skin and eyes, and others that keep your heart pumping and your insides working without you having to think about them.

HOW do muscles work?

When you tense a muscle, it gets shorter and thicker, and pulls on whatever it is attached to. Most muscles work in pairs. For example, you tense the biceps muscle to bend your arm. To straighten your arm, the triceps muscle tenses and the biceps muscle relaxes.

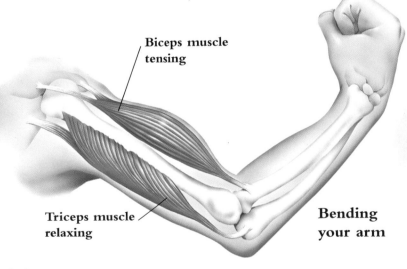

Biceps muscle tensing

Triceps muscle relaxing

Bending your arm

14

WHY do dancers need to warm up?

For muscles to work well, they need a good supply of blood and oxygen. Dancers and athletes do gentle exercises to loosen and stretch

their muscles before they start any exercise. This increases the blood flow to their muscles, giving them more energy. If you exercise hard without warming up, you risk getting painful cramps or you may strain and injure your muscles.

That's Amazing!

Nearly half your body weight is made up of muscles!

You use eight to twelve different muscles in your face just to smile!

Now I Know...

★ Every movement of your body is made by muscles.
★ Muscles work by pulling on parts of the body.
★ Dancers warm up to increase the blood flow to their muscles.

★ Look and Find ★

platelet

HOW does blood flow?

Blood flows around your body all the time, carrying oxygen and food to every cell and taking away **waste**. Your blood is pumped along by the heart, an organ with strong walls of muscle. First, the blood is sent to your lungs to collect oxygen, then it returns to your heart and is pumped to the rest of your body. The tubes that carry blood away from the heart are called **arteries**. Those that carry blood back to the heart are called **veins**.

Vein carrying blood from the upper body

WHAT is blood made of?

More than half of your blood is made of a pale liquid called plasma. Floating in it are red cells, white cells and platelets. Billions of saucer-shaped red cells carry oxygen around your body. Different types of white cells fight **germs**, to protect your body from infection. Tiny platelets help your blood to clot and form a scab if you cut yourself and bleed.

Vein carrying blood from the lower body

White cell

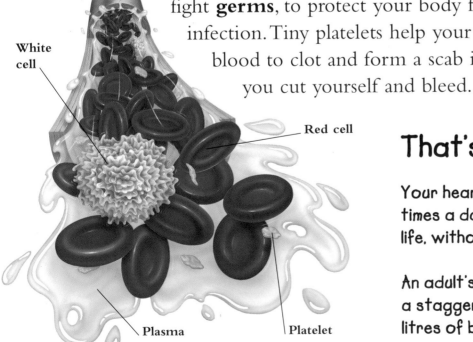

Red cell

Plasma

Platelet

That's Amazing!

Your heart beats about 100,000 times a day, every day of your life, without getting tired!

An adult's heart pumps a staggering 15,000 litres of blood a day!

Artery carrying blood to the body

Artery carrying blood to the lungs

WHY does your heart sometimes beat fast?

When you cycle or do any other exercise, your muscles need extra oxygen to give you more energy. Your brain sends signals to your heart, which beats harder and faster to pump more blood to your muscles. You also breathe faster to take in more oxygen, so there is more oxygen in your blood.

The heart and kidneys

Heart

Kidneys remove any chemicals in blood that the body does not need

Arteries and veins supply the heart itself with blood

Now I Know...

★ Your heart pumps blood around your body non-stop.

★ Blood is made of plasma, red cells, white cells and platelets.

★ Your heart beats faster when you need extra energy.

HOW do you breathe?

You breathe automatically because your body needs a gas called oxygen to stay alive. Your lungs are like two sponges full of tiny air tubes which branch off from your windpipe. When you breathe in, your lungs swell up as air fills the tubes. Oxygen passes out of the tubes into your blood to travel around your body. At the same time, a waste gas called **carbon dioxide** passes from your blood into your lungs. Your lungs shrink again as you breathe air out.

WHAT does your nose do?

You breathe in air through your nose and down your windpipe to your lungs. Your nose warms the air you breathe in. **Mucus** and hairs inside it also trap dirt to stop it reaching your lungs. A small area at the top of your nose is full of nerve cells that detect smells in the air. These give you your sense of smell.

Air is breathed in through your nose

Air travels down your windpipe

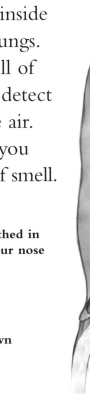

Windpipe

Right lung

The lungs

Left lung is smaller than the right to make room for the heart

Left lung

Air tubes inside the lung

Diaphragm – a sheet of muscle

WHY do people cough?

If dust, germs or mucus get into your windpipe or the air tubes in your lungs and irritate them, you cough automatically. You take a deep breath and pressure builds up inside your lungs. When you cough, air shoots out of your lungs. The rush of air out of your lungs makes the **vocal cords** in your throat rattle and you hear your cough as a noise. The cough also shoots out dust, germs and mucus along with air.

Now I Know...

★ You breathe automatically because your body needs oxygen to stay alive.

★ Your nose warms the air you breathe in and traps dirt.

★ People cough to get rid of dirt in their windpipe or lungs.

19

HOW do you see?

Your eyes pick up light that is reflected from whatever you look at. They send signals to your brain telling you what you see. The light bends as it goes through the cornea at the front of your eye. It then passes into the eye itself through a hole called the pupil. A lens focuses the light and forms moving images of what you see onto the retina, the back wall of the eye. Millions of light-sensitive cells in the retina then send the images to your brain along the optic nerve.

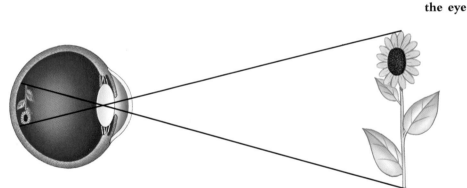

The lens in your eye turns images upside down, but your brain turns them the right way up for you.

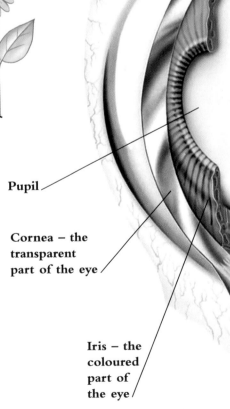

White of the eye

Pupil

Cornea – the transparent part of the eye

Iris – the coloured part of the eye

Lens

WHAT makes you blink?

You blink automatically every two to ten seconds to keep the delicate surface of each eye healthy. When your eyelids close, they spread tear fluid across your eyes to wash away dust and germs, and keep the surface moist.

20

The eyeball

WHY do some people wear glasses?

Many people need glasses or contact lenses to help them see clearly. Some people are short-sighted and cannot focus on distant objects, which look blurred. Other people are long-sighted and cannot focus on things close to them, which in turn look blurred. Contact lenses and the lenses in glasses help to focus images clearly on the retina.

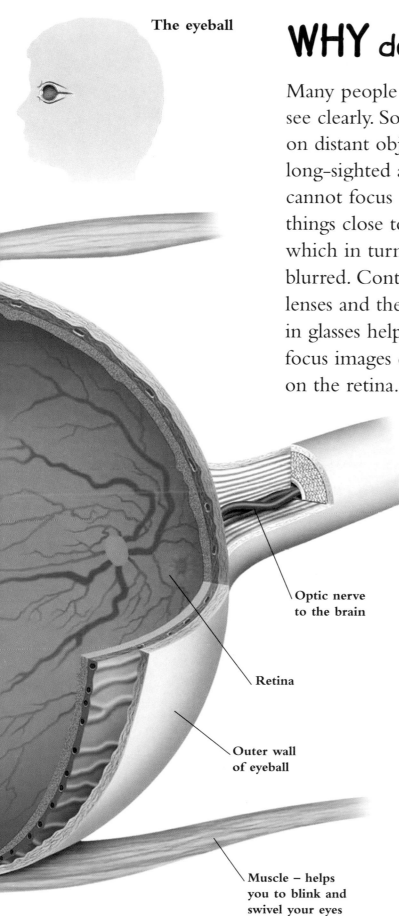

Optic nerve to the brain

Retina

Outer wall of eyeball

Muscle – helps you to blink and swivel your eyes

That's Amazing!

On average, you blink about 10,000 times a day!

You have 200 eyelashes around each eye to keep out dust and grit!

Now I Know...

★ Your eyes and brain work together to help you see.
★ You blink to clean dust and germs out of your eyes.
★ People wear glasses so they can see clearly.

HOW do you hear?

Sounds travel through the air as vibrations called sound waves. Your ears pick up the waves and send signals to your brain. The outer part of each ear carries the sound waves to your ear drum, which vibrates. These vibrations pass along tiny bones to the cochlea. This is a spiral-shaped tube full of liquid deep inside your ear. The liquid moves and triggers tiny hairs that are attached to nerve cells. These send signals to your brain and you hear sounds.

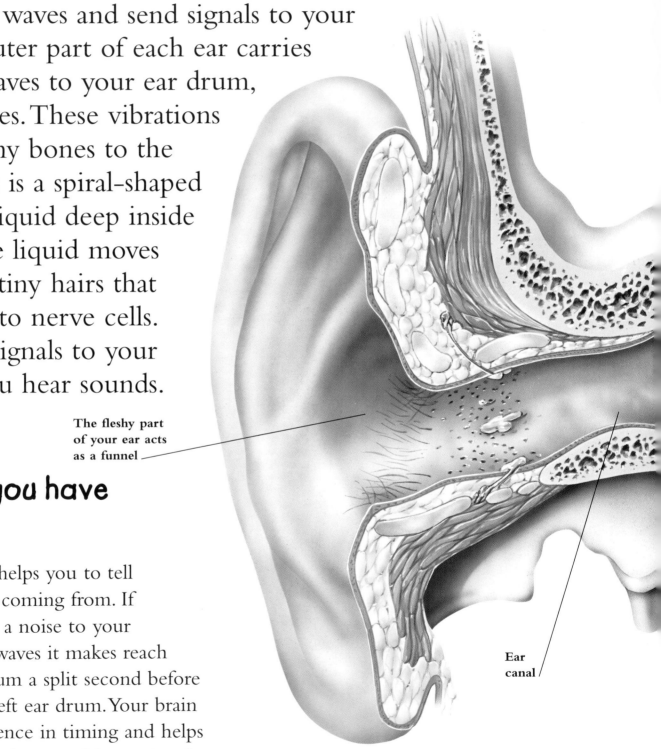

The fleshy part of your ear acts as a funnel

Ear canal

WHY do you have two ears?

Having two ears helps you to tell where a sound is coming from. If something makes a noise to your right, the sound waves it makes reach your right ear drum a split second before they reach your left ear drum. Your brain notices the difference in timing and helps you to tell where the sound is coming from.

The right ear

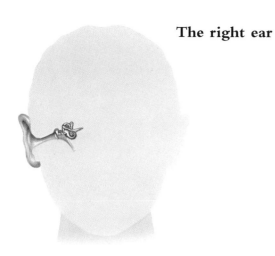

That's Amazing!

You can tell the difference between over 1,500 different tones of sound!

No two people have exactly the same shaped ears!

Semi-circular canals

Nerve leading to brain

Cochlea

Ear drum vibrates like skin on a drum when sound waves hit it

WHAT keeps you balanced?

Your ears help to keep you balanced. There are three tubes called semi-circular canals inside your ear. These contain fluid, and nerve cells connected to tiny hairs. When your head moves, the fluid and hairs in the tubes move. This sends nerve signals to your brain, telling you if you are upright.

Now I Know...

★ Your ears pick up sound waves in the air so you can hear.

★ Having two ears helps you to judge where sounds come from.

★ Your ears help to keep you balanced.

23

WHY do you need to eat?

You cannot live without food. It gives you energy and makes you grow. Eating different foods also keeps you healthy and helps you to get better if you are ill or have hurt yourself. Before your body can use the food you eat, it has to be broken down into tiny pieces, so that useful bits called **nutrients** are small enough to pass into your blood. This process is called digestion. Your digestive system starts in your mouth. It is made up of several organs that take it in turn to break down the food you eat.

Liver – organ that sorts out nutrients after they have been through the small intestine

WHERE does food go?

Your teeth and **saliva** break down food in your mouth. Once you have swallowed the food, it is squeezed down a tube called the gullet to your stomach. There it is churned up and mixed with chemicals to make a thick soup. This mixture is squeezed slowly along a long, wiggly tube called the small intestine. Nutrients pass through its thin walls into your blood to go round your body. The remaining food travels to your large intestine, which soaks up water. Solid wastes are stored in your rectum until you go to the toilet.

That's Amazing!

On average, a person eats 30 tonnes of food and drinks 50,000 litres of liquid during their lifetime!

Your tongue has more than 10,000 taste buds on its surface!

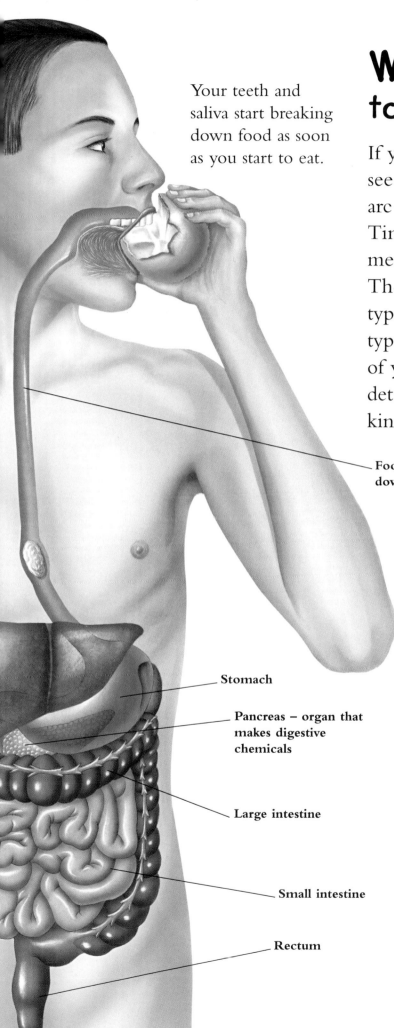

Your teeth and saliva start breaking down food as soon as you start to eat.

Food travels down gullet

Stomach

Pancreas – organ that makes digestive chemicals

Large intestine

Small intestine

Rectum

WHY is the surface of your tongue bumpy?

If you look at your tongue in a mirror, you can see small bumps on it. Around each bump there arc taste buds. These give you your sense of taste. Tiny sense cells in them detect flavours and send messages to your brain, which identifies them. There are four different types of taste bud. Each type is on a different part of your tongue and detects a particular kind of taste.

Bitter taste

Sour taste

Salty taste

Sweet taste

Now I Know...

★ Food gives you energy, makes you grow and keeps you healthy.

★ Food travels through organs in your digestive system.

★ The surface of your tongue is covered with bumpy tastebuds.

WHERE do babies come from?

Women have egg cells inside them and men have sperm cells. Both are needed to make a baby. Every baby starts life as a tiny egg smaller than a full stop. The egg is made when a man and woman make love. They cuddle and lie close together, and the man puts liquid full of sperm cells into the woman. If one of the sperm cells joins an egg cell inside the woman, it settles in the **womb** in her abdomen and a baby starts to grow.

HOW long did you live in your mother's womb?

You lived in your mother's womb for about nine months, living in a bag of warm fluid. You could not eat or breathe by yourself. Instead, you got all your food and oxygen through a tube called the **umbilical cord**, which went from your tummy button to your mother.

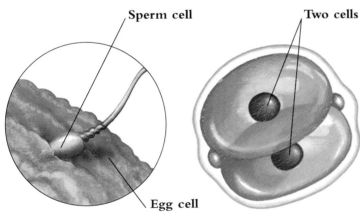

Sperm cell

Egg cell

Two cells

1 Sperm look like tadpoles. When a sperm cell finds an egg cell, it wriggles into it so they are joined together.

2 The egg splits into two cells. They keep dividing, making a ball of cells that grows bigger and bigger.

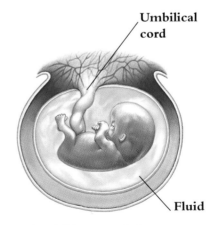

Umbilical cord

Fluid

3 After eight weeks, all the main parts of the baby have formed and it is floating in a bag of fluid.

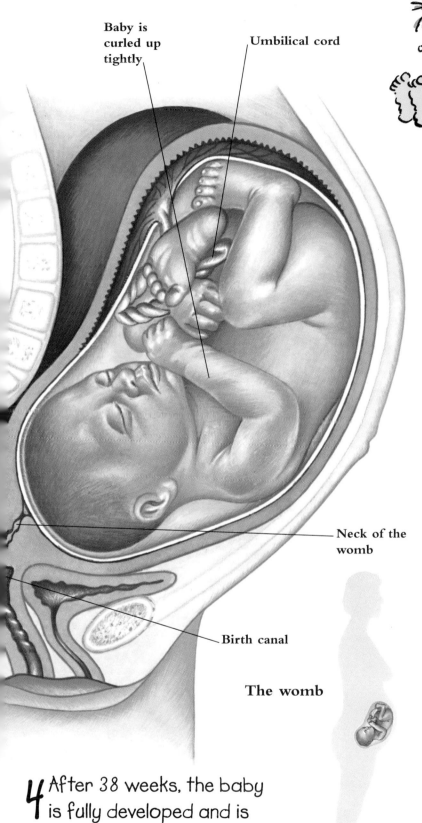

Baby is curled up tightly

Umbilical cord

Neck of the womb

Birth canal

The womb

4 After 38 weeks, the baby is fully developed and is very squashed in the womb. It is usually upside down and is ready to be born.

HOW are babies born?

The muscles in the wall of the womb are very strong. When a baby is ready to be born, these muscles tighten and push the baby down. The neck of the womb slowly opens until it is big enough for the baby's head to go through. The mother's muscles squeeze harder and slowly push the baby along the birth canal and out of her body.

Now I Know...

★ A baby is begun when a man's sperm cell joins a woman's egg cell.

★ You lived in your mother's womb for about nine months.

★ A baby is born when its mother's womb muscles push it out.

WHY can't babies walk and talk?

Babies' muscles are not very strong and they cannot control them very well. They can kick their legs and make sounds, but they do not yet know how to stand up or talk. Babies have to find out what their bodies can do and learn all the basic skills they need for life. They do this by copying other people and trying things out again and again. As you grow up, you spend a lot of time trying out and learning new skills, even when you are playing.

One-year-olds have big heads compared to their bodies, and short arms and legs.

Six-year-olds are much taller. Their bodies are longer compared to their heads.

At 14, people have longer arms and legs. Their bodies look more like adult bodies.

At 20, people are adults. Their bodies are fully grown and developed.

28

HOW do you grow?

When you are a child, the bones inside you grow fast. This changes what you look like. Not all your bones grow at the same time. When you were small, you had a big brain, so the top of your skull was big and your face small. As you grow older, the top of your skull grows only a bit, but your face bones grow more.

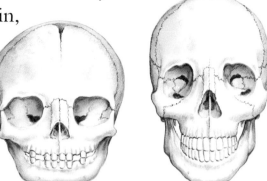

Six-year-old's skull   **16-year-old's skull**

That's Amazing!

Most children recognize 200 words by the time they are two years old!

Our ears carry on growing about 0.22 millimetres a year as we age!

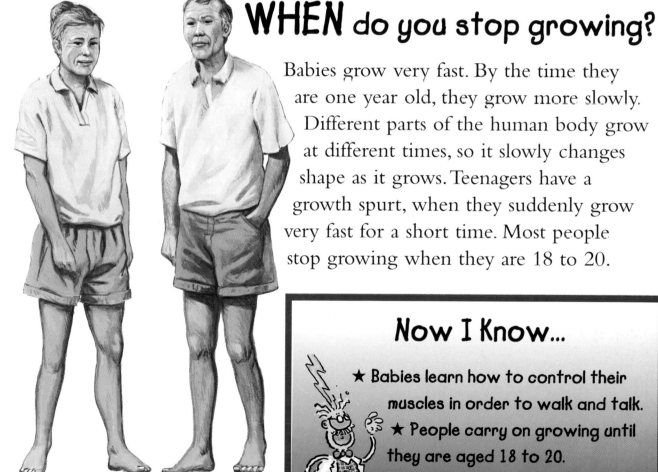

At 60, people are often a bit smaller, with smaller muscles, grey hair and lined skin.

WHEN do you stop growing?

Babies grow very fast. By the time they are one year old, they grow more slowly. Different parts of the human body grow at different times, so it slowly changes shape as it grows. Teenagers have a growth spurt, when they suddenly grow very fast for a short time. Most people stop growing when they are 18 to 20.

Now I Know...

★ Babies learn how to control their muscles in order to walk and talk.
★ People carry on growing until they are aged 18 to 20.
★ You grow because the bones inside you are growing.

HUMAN BODY QUIZ

What have you remembered about the human body? Test what you know and see how much you have learned.

1 What protects your heart and lungs?
a)   your spine
b)   your rib cage
c)   your muscles

2 Which part of your body contains melanin?
a)   your brain
b)   your lungs
c)   your skin

3 What carries messages to and from your brain?
a)   nerves
b)   muscles
c)   bones

4 What makes up your skeleton?
a)   bones
b)   joints
c)   muscles

5 What happens when you tense a muscle?
a)   it gets longer
b)   it gets shorter
c)   it relaxes

6 What carries oxygen around your body?
a)   nerves
b)   blood
c)   food

7 What is the coloured part of your eye called?
a)   the lens
b)   the pupil
c)   the iris

8 Where in your body can you find a cochlea?
a)   in your ear
b)   in your eye
c)   in your brain

9 What goes from your mouth to your stomach?
a)   your small intestine
b)   your windpipe
c)   your gullet

10 Where does a baby grow inside its mother?
a)   her womb
b)   her stomach
c)   her chest

Find the answers on page 32.

GLOSSARY

abdomen The lower half of the main part of your body that contains your kidneys and digestive organs.

arteries Tubes that carry blood from your heart to other parts of your body. The blood they carry is usually full of oxygen.

carbon dioxide A waste gas in the air that your body releases when you breathe out.

cells The tiny living units that make up your body.

dermis The layer in your skin that contains sweat glands, nerves and arteries.

digesting Breaking food down into tiny bits that your body can use.

evaporates Dries up and becomes tiny drops of water vapour in the air.

germs Tiny living things that can get into your body and make you ill.

mucus Slimy liquid in your nose and throat.

muscles Parts of your body that make you move.

nerves Wirelike parts in your body that carry messages to and from the brain and spinal cord.

nutrients Useful parts of food that your body needs for growth, energy and health.

organs Important parts of the body that carry out different roles.

oxygen A gas in the air; you need to breathe it in to live.

pores Tiny holes in your skin.

saliva Spit inside your mouth which contains a chemical that breaks down food.

umbilical cord The tube that joins an unborn baby to its mother's womb.

veins Tubes that carry blood back to your heart. The blood they carry is usually low in oxygen.

vocal cords Two stretchy flaps in your throat that vibrate and make sounds when air passes through them.

waste Leftover food, fluids, gases or chemicals that your body does not need and must get rid of.

womb An organ in a mother's abdomen where an unborn baby grows.

X-ray A type of photograph that shows solid things inside your body, such as bones.

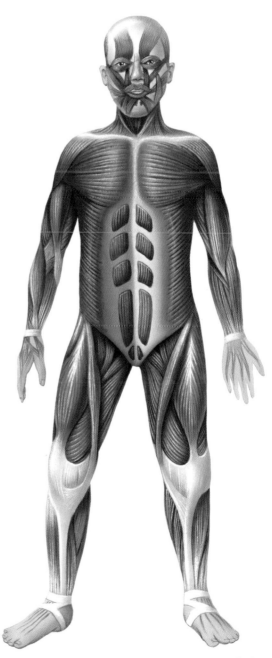

INDEX

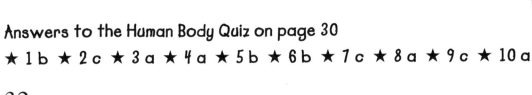

Answers to the Human Body Quiz on page 30

★ 1 b ★ 2 c ★ 3 a ★ 4 a ★ 5 b ★ 6 b ★ 7 c ★ 8 a ★ 9 c ★ 10 a